The New York Times

HAPPY HOLIDAY BOOK OF MINI CROSSWORDS

The New York Times

HAPPY HOLIDAY BOOK OF MINI CROSSWORDS
150 Easy Fun-Sized Puzzles

Joel Fagliano

ST. MARTIN'S GRIFFIN
NEW YORK

First published in the United States by St. Martin's Griffin,
an imprint of St. Martin's Publishing Group

www.stmartins.com

ISBN 978-1-250-22187-2

Our books may be purchased in bulk for promotional, educational, or
business use. Please contact your local bookseller or the Macmillan Corporate
and Premium Sales Department at 1-800-221-7945, extension 5442, or by email at
MacmillanSpecialMarkets@macmillan.com.

First Edition: 2022

10   9   8   7   6   5   4   3   2   1

The New York Times

HAPPY HOLIDAY BOOK OF MINI CROSSWORDS

Introduction

When you think about it, crosswords are particularly well-suited for our fast-paced, modern age. Almost every clue and answer is on a different subject, your mind bounces from one thing to the next, and when a puzzle's not too hard, it takes only a short time to do.

Well, if regular crosswords are modern, *The New York Times*'s Mini crosswords are hypermodern. The clues and answers are just as diverse, but each 5×5-square grid takes a mere minute or so to complete—even less once you get good. You now feel the rush of excitement in finishing a puzzle in a fraction of the time!

Launched in 2014, and originally available only digitally, the Mini has become so popular that now on weekdays it also appears in print in the main section of the paper.

Each Mini is created by Joel Fagliano, the paper's digital crosswords editor, who started selling regular crosswords to the *Times* when he was seventeen. To date he's had more than 50 weekday and Sunday crosswords published in the paper, becoming in the process one of the most popular and accomplished puzzlemakers.

Joel packs his Minis with lively vocabulary, modern references, and the sort of playfulness and intelligence you'll find in its big brother elsewhere in the paper. The Minis are easy/medium in difficulty. The cultural references skew young. But don't let the small size and big squares fool you. These puzzles are decidedly for adults.

On the following pages are 150 Minis from the *Times,* lightly re-edited for their first publication in book form.

Let the many rushes of excitement begin!

—Will Shortz

ACROSS

1 Store with an annual Thanksgiving Day Parade
6 Swell, as a cloud
7 Something made useless by evolution
8 Creation of Congress
9 Wet dirt
10 "Why are you bringing this up to me?"
12 Smith with the most rushing yards in N.F.L. history
13 Witherspoon of "Legally Blonde"

DOWN

1 Do at the wrong moment
2 ___-rock
3 Concern for environmental scientists
4 Dairy product made from cultures
5 Björn Borg or Alexander Skarsgard
6 Turn into
7 Darth ___
11 Prefix with gender, opposite of "trans"

2

	1	2	3	4
	5			
6				
7				
8				

ACROSS

1 First symbol on a musical staff
5 Big name in nutrition bars
6 Plucked string instrument
7 Therefore
8 Like a cakewalk, or a piece of cake

DOWN

1 Santa ____, California
2 They're breathtaking
3 "Have a good time!"
4 ____ Schwarz (toy store)
6 Fuzzy buzzer

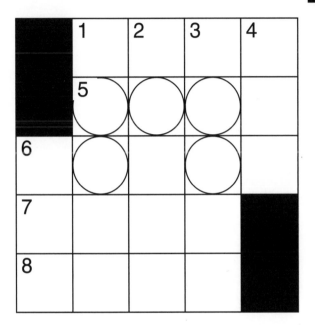

ACROSS

1 Sci-fi crafts
5 Surface for some soccer fields
6 "Beats me"
7 Best Picture winner starring Ben Affleck
8 Bad mood

DOWN

1 Maneuver shown in the circled letters
2 Mushrooms and such
3 ". . . I guess never mind"
4 Bay Area airport, briefly
6 Marx's "____ Kapital"

4

1	2	3	4	■
5				6
7				
8				
■	9			

ACROSS

1 Without delay
5 Run out, as a subscription
7 This Greek letter: α
8 Green energy source
9 ___ Feed (Facebook feature)

DOWN

1 "Woe is me!"
2 Hairdresser's establishment
3 iCloud creator
4 "Nonsense!"
6 Obstacles for barbers

1	2	3	4	5
6				
7				
8				
9			■	■

ACROSS

1 Shinzo Abe's country
6 Brunch offering
7 Like sumo wrestlers and Jabba the Hutt
8 Was a huge fan of
9 Before, in poetry

DOWN

1 Rapper with the 2016 #1 album "4 Your Eyez Only"
2 Ann ____, Michigan
3 Something that annoys
4 Vaulted part of a church
5 Require

6

	1	2	3	4
5				
6				
7				
8				

ACROSS
1 Ear-cleaning swab
5 Feature of San Francisco's Lombard Street, famously
6 "Want to play this round?"
7 Out of the harbor
8 N.B.A. team that plays at Barclays Center

DOWN
1 This mark: "
2 Have faith in
3 Yale, Princeton, etc.
4 Enrique ___ Nieto, Mexican president since 2012
5 Greenish-blue color

ACROSS

1 Main language of Bangkok
5 Weather vane turner
6 Block game that requires steady hands
7 Official language of Pakistan
8 Rented equipment at Aspen

DOWN

1 Modern dance move done in a squat
2 Most-spoken language of India
3 Black ____ (cattle breed)
4 Its capital is Boise: Abbr.
6 Roast beef au ____

ACROSS

1 Floor-washing tool
4 Lord ___, "She Walks in Beauty" poet
6 Held in one's arms, as a toddler
8 Attila, for one
9 Prefix with dermis
10 Fact-filled volume
12 Home to the University of Washington
13 Disney's Ariel, for one

DOWN

1 Country between India and Thailand
2 Chicago airport hub, on luggage tags
3 Italian cornmeal dish
4 Crème ___ (custardy dessert)
5 Kathmandu resident
6 Deep gorge
7 Chopped into small cubes
11 Banking convenience

ACROSS

1 U.S. intelligence org.
4 It's opened for dinner
6 Record of the Year winner at the 2017 Grammys
7 South ___ (African country)
8 Guys

DOWN

1 "Yeah, I mean, that's obvious"
2 Soft leather
3 Book of maps
4 More, in Spanish
5 Egg layer

10

ACROSS

1 Super cool
5 Old record material
7 X, on a shirt tag
8 Truth ____ (interrogation injection)
9 Get checkmated

DOWN

1 Nights before holidays
2 Dot on a computer screen
3 "S.N.L." host's monologue, e.g.
4 Miley of pop music
6 Super uncool

ACROSS

1 Was in first place
4 Trump's education secretary
6 Word after mirror or spitting
7 Gentle reminder
8 ABC's "___ Anatomy"

DOWN

1 Ring-tailed primate
2 Avoid paying, as taxes
3 Pooch
4 When tripled, sound of a
  correct answer
5 Catches sight of

12

1	2	3	4	5
6				
7				
8				
■	9			

ACROSS

1 Greek "S"
6 N.B.A. great Shaquille
7 Intermission follower
8 Iconic N.Y.C. deli seen in the "S.N.L." opening credits
9 A bit of disputin' from Putin

DOWN

1 Marinate
2 Of an ancient Peruvian empire
3 Los Angeles art museum, with "the"
4 Native American corn crop
5 "He's making ___, checking it twice . . ."

	1	2	3	4
	5			
6				
7				■
8				■

ACROSS

1 Tiny whirlpool
5 & 6 Guarantee of the First Amendment
7 Half of a clothing pair
8 Fluids in pens

DOWN

1 Zac of "Dirty Grandpa"
2 Worthless stuff
3 Furniture in a school classroom
4 "Signs point to ___" (Magic 8 Ball answer)
6 Letter before omega

14

ACROSS

1 With 8-Across, loser to "Moonlight" for Best Picture
5 Calf-length skirts
6 Go ___ and beyond
7 Snippet of "Hamilton," e.g.
8 See 1-Across

DOWN

1 Benghazi's country
2 Embellish
3 Really, really mad
4 "Hold on ___!"
5 Shopper's mecca

1	2	3	4	5	6	7
8						
9						
		10				
11	12				13	14
15						
16				17		

ACROSS

1 Something hung over a shower rod to dry

8 Country disputing the annexation of Crimea

9 _____ Jenner, transgender icon

10 James Comey's org.

11 Group of cyclists in a pack

15 Like Napoleon when he was on Elba

16 Makeup of a music collection, once

17 Do some summing

DOWN

1 Tampa Bay football player, for short

2 Letters before an alias

3 Things of little importance

4 Place to store bowlers and bonnets

5 "Well-regulated" thing in the Second Amendment

6 "Pick a number, _____ number"

7 X, in Roman numerals

11 Photo

12 Conclusion

13 Played out

14 Homer's neighbor on "The Simpsons"

16

1	2	3	4	
5				
6				7
	8			
	9			

ACROSS

1 Running bills at the bar
5 Fe, on the periodic table
6 Grammy-winning singer Jones
8 Button clicked to see the rest of an article, maybe
9 Egyptian cross

DOWN

1 Sn, on the periodic table
2 Pleasant smell
3 B, on the periodic table
4 Cynical, mocking humor
7 "That's kinda funny . . ."

ACROSS

1 Recede, as the tide
4 Former F.B.I. director James
6 Not together
7 Notably boring color
8 Show on which Melissa McCarthy played Sean Spicer

DOWN

1 Inbox filler
2 Ice shelf breakoff
3 Computer memory unit
4 Uber competitors
5 Click on, as a 1-Down

18

ACROSS
1 & 5 "Keep being socially aware," in modern slang
6 First, second, third and reverse
7 Mexican currency
8 Abbr. before a name on a memo

DOWN
1 Short and ___
2 "Here's to the happy couple," e.g.
3 Ohio city where LeBron James was born
4 "Totally agree"
6 Valedictorian's pride, for short

ACROSS

1 The "P" of PRNDL
5 "Breaking Bad" or "Mad Men," genrewise
7 ___ position (curled-up state)
8 Go "Zzzzz"
9 Hill-building insects

DOWN

1 Many emailed files
2 Basketball venue
3 Boca ___, Florida
4 Target competitor
6 Microbrewery creations

20

ACROSS

1 Texter's "That's incredible!"
4 Each and ___
6 Device with an AM-FM switch
7 European country where the 8-Across was invented
8 Instrument that's straddled while played

DOWN

1 Egg-shaped
2 Prize at the Olympics
3 Cook on the barbecue
4 ___ Garcetti, mayor of Los Angeles
5 Ma who plays the 8-Across

1	2	3	4	5
6				
7				
8				
9				

ACROSS

1 Desert animal with three eyelids
6 Modern prefix with care
7 2017 box office hit about Wolverine
8 Garment of ancient Greece
9 Lacking crunch, as potato chips

DOWN

1 Indianapolis football team
2 What "~" means when seen before a number
3 ___ Carta
4 Bad thing to check on vacation
5 Weapon for a knight

22

ACROSS
1 401(k) alternatives
5 Hurried
8 Comedian Aziz
9 "What's up?," in Spanish
11 Light-refracting devices
12 Watch illegally over the internet, maybe
13 Paris airport

DOWN
1 Country excluded from the second iteration of Trump's travel ban
2 Periods preceding big events
3 Claim with conviction
4 Ari ___, host of NPR's "All Things Considered"
6 Pink side of a pencil
7 Pitifully bad
10 "___ mother used to say . . ."

ACROSS

1 Rock blaster
4 Income increaser
7 One with a jaded outlook on life
8 Alcohol, slangily
9 Boxing ref's decision

DOWN

1 Geological formation on Utah's state license plate
2 B.L.T. ingredient
3 ___ noir (red wine grape)
5 Under the weather
6 Home device from Amazon

	1	2	3
4	5		
6			
7			
8			

ACROSS

1 Spy org
4 Admirer of Beauty, with "the"
6 Marco of the U.S. Senate
7 Come up
8 Prefix with profit

DOWN

1 Lincoln was born in one
2 Egyptian fertility goddess
3 Stick ___ in the water
4 Muffin ingredient
5 Coin used since 2002

ACROSS

1 Little chirp
5 Something a Boy Scout earns
6 One working on labor day?
7 Hits open-handed
8 Put into piles, as laundry

DOWN

1 "The Life of ___," #1 album for Kanye West
2 Painter Degas
3 Home to the Great Sphinx of Giza
4 Ballpoints, e.g.
5 One side of a raise negotiation

26

ACROSS
1 Take a plane
4 ___ Navidad
6 Rapper whose real name is Aubrey Graham
7 Japanese noodle soup
8 The "L" of U.N.L.V.

DOWN
1 Wild, as an animal
2 Animal that will spit on you when agitated
3 "That ain't pretty"
4 President on the dime, for short
5 Branch of Buddhism

ACROSS
1 Dr. Frankenstein's workplace
4 Semester-ending tests
7 Pond scum
8 Jordan who directed "Get Out"
9 Conducted

DOWN
1 ___ of faith
2 Rod connecting car wheels
3 Roll with a hole
5 M, on an application
6 Sesame ___ (3-Down topper)

1	2	3	4	5
6				
7				
8				
9				

ACROSS

1 Clicks "Going" on a Facebook event, e.g.
6 In the know
7 "I kid you not!"
8 Meaning of the slang words "turnt" and "lit"
9 Red root vegetables

DOWN

1 Genre for R. Kelly or Luther Vandross
2 Used cusswords
3 Think highly of
4 Make a paper copy of
5 Tries to locate

ACROSS

1 "____ we forget . . ."
5 Allen Iverson or Dr. J, once
6 Woodstock attendee
7 Wells Fargo or Citigroup
8 Showily decorated
9 "Green-winged" ducks
10 Captain's place on a ship

DOWN

1 ChapStick, e.g.
2 Former residents now living overseas, informally
3 River that passes by the Louvre
4 "Star ____ Beyond" (2016 sci-fi movie)
5 Cue
6 One recently put on the payroll
7 Best of ____ worlds

	1	2	3
4 / 5			
6			
7			
8			

ACROSS

1 Government org. in NBC's "The Blacklist"
4 "Go ahead, what's your question?"
6 Tennis setting
7 Bowling setting
8 "N.Y. State of Mind" rapper

DOWN

1 They lead to free throws
2 ___ to tears
3 Tiny, informally
4 Read, as a bar code
5 Hello, in Honduras

ACROSS

1 "Jane ___," Brontë novel
5 Group of March Madness brackets
6 Portend
8 Like talking loudly on your phone on the train
9 Ranking in March Madness

DOWN

1 Green branch, for short
2 Not mine
3 Going ___ (disobeying directions)
4 Escape the grasp of
7 One side in checkers

32

	1	2	3	4
	5			
6				
7				
8				

ACROSS

1 Apple computers
5 ___ vera
6 Trail behind a snail
7 Something a million times smaller than a human hair
8 "S.N.L." alum Carvey

DOWN

1 Smallest country in the European Union
2 "March comes in like ___ . . ."
3 ,
4 "You get my point?"
6 Tear-jerking

ACROSS

1 Grp. that defends civil rights
5 Horned African mammal
7 Boyfriend who checks all the boxes, say
8 Boring
9 Broadway backgrounds

DOWN

1 Half of the McDonald's logo
2 Complete pandemonium
3 Flexible, as a dancer's body
4 Not edited
6 ___ law (physics class topic)

34

¹	²	³	■	■
⁴			⁵	⁶
⁷				
⁸				
■	⁹			

ACROSS

1 With 3-Down,
   ultra-conservative bloc
4 Straighten
7 Church doctrine
8 Values of a community
9 Airport screening org.

DOWN

1 Tapering haircut
2 Tons
3 See 1-Across
5 Biologically engineered crops,
   as they're often called
6 "Houston, we have a problem"
   grp.

	1	2	3	4
5				
6				
7				
8				

ACROSS

1 This means nothing
5 Many a Google employee
6 Squabble
7 Reporters, with "the"
8 What glasses rest on

DOWN

1 Famous swordsman with a "Z" cut
2 A cube has twelve while a sphere has none
3 Decide not to throw away
4 Mined metals
5 ___ Crunch (cereal mascot)

ACROSS

1 Nissan Rogue or Ford Escape
4 "Shut up!"
6 Inn crowd?
8 "An object in motion stays in motion" concept
9 Beirut is its capital
10 Fathers, in babyspeak
11 Sleep phase, briefly

DOWN

1 Where the Trending section on Facebook is found
2 Software improvement
3 Setting for "Apocalypse Now"
4 Divided, as urban real estate
5 Three-part bands
6 Rap's _____ Wayne
7 _____ Diego, CA

ACROSS

1 "Six-pack" muscles
4 Device used to make whiskey
6 International Court of Justice site, with "the"
7 Felt sore
8 Like ghost peppers

DOWN

1 "Sure," slangily
2 Democratic, on a political map
3 Iditarod vehicle
4 Onetime head of Iran
5 ___ truck (Mexican street vendor)

1	2	3	4	5
6				
7				
8				
9				■

ACROSS

1 Bed-facing item in a hotel room
6 "Bonjour" or "Ciao"
7 Fishing line holders
8 Fencing swords
9 Fox Sports 1 competitor

DOWN

1 A one and a two
2 Biden and Pence, slangily
3 Something a new parent craves
4 Actress Barkin
5 Flip, as a coin

ACROSS

1 Boxer Muhammad
4 Sub maker
6 Group of three
8 Sub maker
9 Reason for a TV-MA rating

DOWN

1 Insect in a colony
2 Animal fat
3 Prestigious group of U.S. schools
5 One of the 3-Down
7 French for "ten"

40

ACROSS

1 Recently retired Monopoly piece (along with the thimble and wheelbarrow)
5 Divide into two equal parts
6 ___ finger, between the thumb and middle
7 Work period of limited duration
8 Takes to court

DOWN

1 African language from which "marimba" and "gumbo" come
2 1960s song, now
3 Pizza cookers
4 Cause of a pocket buzz
5 Sound of a snake or leaking tire

ACROSS

1 Salsa option
5 Neighbor of Pennsylvania
6 Out of money
7 Rock climber's equipment
8 Tip jar bills

DOWN

1 Doofus
2 [Crossing my fingers]
3 Support for a Facebook post
4 Mother of a fawn
6 Dude

42

ACROSS

1 Big truck maker
5 Currency of 19 countries
6 Kushner in the Trump White House
7 Entrance to a tent
8 "S.N.L." cast member Mooney

DOWN

1 Like the consistency of an old apple
2 Hearing-related
3 Thin pancake
4 Down for the count, informally
6 N.Y.C. airport

ACROSS

1 ___ generis
4 Channel that receives N.E.A. funding
7 Jake Tapper's employer
8 Giants QB Manning
9 Get food delivered
11 Rife (with)
12 Area of expertise for an I.R.S. auditor
13 Monopoly cards
14 ___ Moines, Iowa

DOWN

1 Brand of toilet paper
2 Like emails that are in bold
3 Intended to mirror the market, as a fund
4 . . . .
5 Adjustable window coverings
6 Lightly burn
10 Oscars host, e.g.

ACROSS

1 Seasoning on an everything bagel
5 Veggie bit on an everything bagel
7 Seed on an everything bagel
8 Adjective follower
9 Undercover agent

DOWN

1 Soak (up)
2 Unknown author: Abbr.
3 Weight loss surgeries, informally
4 Refresh, as a cup of coffee
6 Home to many bagel shops, for short

ACROSS

1 Something in a game of Yankee Swap
5 Foul-smelling
7 Home to baseball's Marlins
8 Neighbor of Saudi Arabia
9 Start over from scratch

DOWN

1 Adjective used to describe venison
2 More slippery, as winter roads
3 One-tenth of a bowling game
4 Used a stopwatch on
6 T. rex, e.g.

46

ACROSS

1 In support of
4 ←
5 Old West trading posts
6 Nectar collectors
7 Govt. agency that's busy this time of year

DOWN

1 Shouts after errant golf shots
2 Ins and ___
3 $200 Monopoly properties: Abbr.
4 Author Jonathan Safran ___
5 J. Edgar Hoover's org.

1	2	3	4	5
6				
7				
8				
9				

ACROSS

1 Overly sentimental
6 Share the same opinion
7 Truckers shift them frequently
8 ___ the Giant, pro wrestling legend
9 Remains

DOWN

1 Long, drawn-out tales
2 Recipient of thanks in an Oscars acceptance speech
3 "The Devil Wears ___"
4 Trump energy secretary Rick
5 Thumbs-up votes

48

ACROSS

1 Chill (with)
5 Capital of Afghanistan
6 Ultraviolet ray blocker in the stratosphere
7 Bank that stops flooding
8 Microbrewery brews

DOWN

1 Greenish-brown eye color
2 On top of
3 Devin _____, former chairman of the House Intelligence Committee
4 Mirth
5 Nut that contains caffeine

ACROSS

1 Ponzi scheme, for one
5 Programmer's output
6 One of the Great Lakes
7 "Right away!"
8 Leave at the altar

DOWN

1 Italian "Pardon me . . ."
2 Reef material
3 Get an animal from the shelter
4 Nearly all users of the app Grindr
6 Journey to Mecca

ACROSS

1 "Toucan play that game," e.g.
4 Out of bed
6 Something a reporter scribbles on
8 Alphabet starter
9 ____ TV (channel airing March Madness games)
10 Neil on the Supreme Court
12 Rebellious years, often
13 Tiny

DOWN

1 Tire-changing NASCAR group
2 Exploit
3 Planet with recorded wind speeds of 1,300 mph
4 Cyborg = human + ____
5 Anti-drug cops
6 Be a noodge
7 "It's so obvious now!"
11 Go on dates with

ACROSS

1 Alternative to an Uber or Lyft
4 & 6 Award won by Einstein, Churchill and Sartre
7 Dangerous noble gas
8 French article

DOWN

1 Barrier reef makeup
2 Put up with
3 Amazon head Jeff
4 "All Things Considered" airer
5 "Dancing With the Stars" judge Goodman

52

	1	2	3	
4				5
6				
7				
	8			

ACROSS

1 Silent signal of comprehension
4 Amazon C.E.O. Jeff
6 Like teddy bears and bad radio reception
7 Fast food side order
8 Massive Brit. reference work

DOWN

1 Study of the brain, casually
2 Baseball's Smith or Guillén
3 Took a nap
4 Favorite texting partner, for short
5 The "S" of GPS: Abbr.

1	2	3	4	5
6				
7				
8				
■	9			■

ACROSS

1 "How disappointing!"
6 Lying facedown
7 One of Columbus's ships
8 Meal at which to drink Manischewitz wine
9 Color of Manischewitz wine

DOWN

1 Uber and Lyft, e.g.
2 More dry, as humor
3 Paris newspaper Le _____
4 Chipped in poker chips
5 Close by

ACROSS

1 With 3-Down, jack, queen and king
5 Hold a rock climber's rope
6 Love to pieces
7 Curves in the road
8 Former spouses

DOWN

1 UPS rival
2 Without anyone else
3 See 1-Across
4 Easy on the ___
5 Sheep-herding pig of film

ACROSS

1 Org. for the Suns and Heat
4 "The Tortoise and the Hare" storyteller
7 Company with a much-derided protest ad
8 "Give it ___!"
9 Refusals

DOWN

1 California wine valley
2 Sommelier : wine :: cicerone : ___
3 Colorado ski resort
5 ___ buco (veal dish)
6 Parts of peaches

56

ACROSS

1 With 8-Across, Best Actress winner for "La La Land"
5 One of the seven fruits in Hawaiian Punch
7 Best Actress, e.g.
8 See 1-Across
9 Six-footed scurriers

DOWN

1 Many celebrities have big ones
2 Slangy verb akin to coulda or shoulda
3 City in central Georgia
4 ___-garde theatre
6 Greek god of war

ACROSS

1 Thrilla in Manila boxer
4 ___ plug (part of an engine)
6 Hits an infield fly
8 Florida home to Walt Disney World
9 Mammal seen off the California coast
10 List included with a board game
11 ___ Moines, Iowa

DOWN

1 Clap as a crowd
2 Catholic university in Philadelphia
3 Humorous contradictions
4 More achy
5 High praise
6 Counterpart of neg.
7 Heavy weight

58

	1	2	3	
4				5
6				
7				
8				

ACROSS

1 &

4 Something a meteorologist tracks

6 Hasbro game with an off-limits word

7 Apportion

8 Written symbol carved in stone

DOWN

1 Even a little bit

2 In a high-minded manner

3 Sag

4 Deer sir?

5 Insect flitting around a flame

	1	2	3	4
	5			
6				
7				
8				

ACROSS

1 Missiles and bombs
5 & 6 Slangy term for something unimpressive
7 "___ You Were Trouble," 2012 hit for Taylor Swift
8 Requirements

DOWN

1 No longer sleeping
2 Get together with old classmates
3 Sprayed, as a mugger
4 Depicts in a biased way
6 Greed, pride or envy

60

ACROSS

1 2 + 4 + 6, e.g.
4 Pond vessel
6 Luggage attachment
7 Broken arm holder
8 Nay's opposite

DOWN

1 "Sorry to say . . ."
2 Loosen, as laces
3 Disney film featuring the shapeshifting demigod Maui
4 "___ for Cookie" ("Sesame Street" song)
5 Omelet ingredient

ACROSS

1 Animal house
5 Spoil
6 Sudden increase in voltage
7 One of the Four Corners states
8 Sleeveless piece of clothing

DOWN

1 "Et tu, ____?"
2 Surrounding glows
3 Conservatives, with "the"
4 Philly-to-N.Y.C. direction: Abbr.
6 Gas-guzzling car, maybe

62

1	2	3	4	5
6				
7				
8				
9				

ACROSS

1 Two-in-one utensil
6 ___ Missile Crisis
7 Desert plant
8 Greek city where Hercules slew the lion, in myth
9 Not be overturned on appeal

DOWN

1 CAT and MRI, e.g.
2 Sound of Seattle
3 ___ Era (2008–16)
4 Bird that quoth "Nevermore"
5 Work, as dough

1	2	3	4	5
6				
7				
8				
9				

ACROSS

1 Path around the sun
6 Common cancer treatment, for short
7 :
8 Bring together
9 Habitats for tropical fish

DOWN

1 Take place
2 River that passes through Lyon
3 Contradict
4 "See ya later!"
5 Awards for Broadway plays

64

ACROSS

1 Teacher fill-ins, informally
5 "___ to ___" (party game)
7 Geological epoch when human ancestors diverged from chimp ancestors
8 "It's cold in here!"
9 Golfer Michelle
10 Where you might see "X is for Xylophone" or "Z is for Zebra"
12 S, on the periodic table
13 Skillful

DOWN

1 Website with timed trivia quizzes
2 Bars read in checkout lanes: Abbr.
3 Extinguished, as a flame
4 Prom attendee
5 1997 film about a basketball-playing dog
6 Hide and ___
7 Degrees for C.E.O.'s
11 Close buddy, slangily

ACROSS

1 Successful dissertation
  defenders
5 Baseball game delayer
6 McCarthy's "The Road" or
  Kerouac's "On the Road"
7 Help with a crime
8 Mercedes-___

DOWN

1 Voyager 2, for one
2 Safe space
3 ___ & Watson (big name in
  deli foods)
4 Michael Che's show, for short
6 Catch

66

ACROSS
1 "Steady as ____ goes"
4 One way to express feeling in a text message
6 Far-right candidate in the French elections
7 Frisbee thrower's wrist movement
8 Channel airing the N.B.A. playoffs

DOWN
1 Refine, as metal
2 Join midway through
3 Pop out, as a DVD
4 Santa's helper
5 Tattoo parlor supply

ACROSS

1 Cigarette dropping
4 Run, as colors
7 About, date-wise
8 Word before bank or whale
9 Space heater?

DOWN

1 Kindergarten basics
2 Lose one's footing
3 "___ the thing . . ."
5 Light beige
6 2017 #1 album for Kendrick Lamar

68

ACROSS
1 Like a neat bed
5 "Unfortunately . . ."
6 Dutch flower
7 Flower that shares its name with part of the eye
8 Abbr. in a Manhattan address

DOWN
1 Daytime host Povich
2 "It's ___ a day's work"
3 Flower that's also a woman's name
4 Psychic's skill, briefly
6 Container for breath mints

69

ACROSS
1 24-packs of beer
6 World's largest tech company
7 Papaya or casaba
8 Actor Colin of "Love Actually"
9 "If all ___ fails . . ."

DOWN
1 ___ latte (Starbucks order)
2 Earth Day month
3 San Antonio team
4 Like the 1%-ers
5 Late night host Meyers

70

ACROSS

1 Tap out, as a telephone number
5 One of 100 in Winnie-the-Pooh's wood
6 100 on a football field
8 Not on time
9 French city near the Swiss border

DOWN

1 Calendar box
2 Matching declaration in poker
3 Assortment
4 Resulted in
7 One of 100 on the Hill: Abbr.

ACROSS

1 Symbol-matching card game
4 iPod contents
6 They fall between Geminis and Leos
8 Condition with repetitive behaviors, for short
9 Sam-___ (Seuss character)
10 Huffington who founded The Huffington Post
12 Kitchen device that dings
13 Alec Baldwin has been one 17 times

DOWN

1 Time-teller in ancient times
2 Key in the upper-left
3 Connect with
4 Finalist with Le Pen in the French elections
5 Construction site sights
6 Paint layers
7 Like a genius
11 ___ Wednesday

72

ACROSS

1 Creatures said to be wise
5 Complete mayhem
7 Automaker based in Palo Alto, Calif.
8 Either of two "Full House" actresses
9 Model's stance

DOWN

1 Eight: Prefix
2 Term for a young dog or seal
3 Cow-catching rope
4 They're always getting stepped on
6 Not crazy

ACROSS

1 A snit is a bad one
5 End-of-semester event
6 Vessels for whitewater rapids
7 Senator Orrin Hatch's state
8 Y.M.C.A. facilities

DOWN

1 Full of nuance, as an acting role
2 Global poverty org.
3 Solemn vows
4 Private Twitter posts, for short
6 It "really tied the room together," in the movie "The Big Lebowski"

74

ACROSS

1 Stupid
5 Company co-founded by Travis Kalanick
6 Extinct birds that are synonymous with "stupid"
8 Part of a sausage chain
9 Move from gate to runway

DOWN

1 Failure
2 Letter-shaped piece of hardware
3 Attendees of the White House Correspondents' Dinner
4 Home to New York City's zoo
7 Go down the bunny slope

ACROSS

1 Something twisted by a wrench
4 Camel's drinking place
6 Chinese greeting
7 Each's partner
8 Period in history

DOWN

1 Not schooled in the ways of the world
2 "Love in this Club" singer, 2008
3 Princess's headgear
4 Number that's its own square root
5 What miso is made of

76

ACROSS

1 Words per clue in this puzzle
4 Cries from magicians after performing tricks
6 Siri, but for the Amazon Echo
7 Competitor of Microsoft Outlook or Yahoo
8 Dip often served with tortilla chips

DOWN

1 Actress Hayek who played Frida Kahlo
2 Just the way it should be
3 Horizontal reference line on a graph
4 Identifies, as on a Facebook photo
5 Part of a house, to José

ACROSS

1 Musical genre for No Doubt or Sublime
4 Coffee grinder input
6 Main branch of a tree
7 Put an end to, as a fight
8 Ignited

DOWN

1 Capital of South Korea
2 One of the Hawaiian islands
3 Predominant emotion in emo song lyrics
4 Potato chip flavor, for short
5 Quieting sound

ACROSS

1 State a point of view
6 Gold digger
7 Put a price on one's freedom
9 Montana's neighbor to the north
10 Counterpart of spays
11 Books of maps
12 Communication system for the deaf: Abbr.
13 Lao-tzu's philosophy

DOWN

1 Brunch dishes served folded over
2 Cuban-American rapper with two #1 hits
3 Still being tested, as an app
4 Closest
5 Country on the Horn of Africa
7 Capital of Yemen
8 Rope thrown by a cowboy

ACROSS

1 Animal on California's state flag
5 Word before Roger or Rancher
6 Bring together into one
7 Biblical betrayer
8 ___ interface

DOWN

1 Paycheck extra
2 Say "y'all" instead of "you all," e.g.
3 Place for wedding vows
4 Some whiskeys
5 "___ On That Beat" (viral dance of 2016)

1	2	3	4	5
6				
7				
8				
9				

ACROSS

1 Cat calls
6 Diddly-___ (nothing)
7 Bonkers
8 Negative media attention
9 Go out of business

DOWN

1 "Morning Joe" network
2 Like the fractions 5/8 and 30/48
3 One-up
4 Yellow jackets, e.g.
5 Walmart or Kmart

ACROSS

1 Slump
4 Feature of an ID card
7 Thespian
8 Ancient Mexican civilization
9 "Much ___ About Nothing"

DOWN

1 Emails with suspicious attachments, e.g.
2 2017 bill that attempted to overhaul the medical system, for short
3 "You've been caught!"
5 A polliwog is a baby one
6 Approximately

82

ACROSS

1 Insolent talk
5 Out the ___ (in great quantities)
6 Permeate
7 Perceives by touch
8 Gets on the nerves of

DOWN

1 Xbox user
2 Resident - or language - of a western Asian country
3 Sends to the free throw line
4 Enemies
5 Coffee shop convenience for a laptop user

ACROSS

1 It's faced during the Pledge of Allegiance
5 Second-largest city in Africa, with roughly 20 million people
6 Item often dropped on Wile E. Coyote
7 Knight's horse
8 Units of corn

DOWN

1 Orange soda brand
2 "What am I, chopped ____?"
3 Zodiac sign
4 Treasure chest contents
5 iPhone protector

84

1	2	3	4	5
6				
7				
8				
9				

ACROSS

1 Federer's rival
6 All by oneself
7 Justice Sotomayor
8 Heavy blow
9 Sally ___, former U.S. attorney general

DOWN

1 Mean, mean, mean
2 Hawaiian greeting
3 Food for a police officer, stereotypically
4 Cartoon style for Pokémon cards
5 By ___ and bounds

85

	1	2	3	4	5	
6						7
8						
9			■	10		
11			12			
13						
■	14				■	

ACROSS
1 ___ by chocolate (rich dessert)
6 2016 Best Picture nominee about aliens
8 It has cities named Athens and Rome
9 President after F.D.R.
10 Container for ashes
11 Utterly ridiculous
13 Leaves the Union
14 Bob of "Full House"

DOWN
1 Puts on fancy clothes, with "up"
2 "Fifty Shades of Grey" genre
3 Balloon filler
4 Magazine with local listings
5 Headgear in a cafeteria
6 Turkish titles
7 They're found between shoulders
12 Opposite of pos.

ACROSS

1 Sleepover wear
4 Completely by chance
6 ___ Cornish, co-host of NPR's "All Things Considered"
7 Use one's nose
8 Game for little sluggers

DOWN

1 Test, as the depth of water
2 Roman province where Jesus was born
3 Talent
4 "Life comes at you ___"
5 Opposite of whisper

ACROSS

1 Grown-up kid?
5 Command-Z, on a Mac
6 Give a call, slangily
7 Airline to Israel
8 Cried

DOWN

1 Shrewdness
2 Like beer that's not in a bottle
3 Grown-up
4 Word before banana or brass
6 Chop down

88

ACROSS

1 Slight advantage
5 Co-author of "The Communist Manifesto"
6 Leave a 0% tip for
8 Napoleon's isle of exile
9 Narrow opening

DOWN

1 Middle of summer?
2 Palm tree fruits
3 Bar and ___
4 Like James Comey, now
7 What the "Gras" of Mardi Gras means

ACROSS

1 Electrical unit
4 Late bedtime
6 Make a pained expression
7 Train that doesn't skip any stops
8 Word before England or Mexico

DOWN

1 Source of the headline "Fall Canceled After 3 Billion Seasons," with "the"
2 Therefore
3 Colorful parrot
4 Hogwarts bird
5 Filmmaker Brooks

ACROSS

1 Have an influence on, as a voter
5 Texter's reaction to a joke
6 Short race, informally
7 Geometry calculation
8 One asking for extra homework, maybe

DOWN

1 Hobbits' home, with "the"
2 Vacillate
3 Construction ___ (road sign)
4 Talk and talk and talk
6 Ballpark figure

ACROSS

1 Blue party, for short
5 Quintet in the word "facetious"
6 Use as a bed
7 ___ gras
8 Say yes silently

DOWN

1 Athlete Sanders nicknamed "Prime Time"
2 Children's song refrain . . . with a hint to this puzzle's central nine squares
3 Mimicked a cow
4 Yellow blazer
5 Sitcom alien

ACROSS

1 Goes back out, as the tide
5 & 6 Clever person
7 Birth rite
8 "That's my guess, anyway"
9 Getting an A+ on
10 Thick carpet style

DOWN

1 Hamming it up
2 ___ soda (brownie ingredient)
3 Fast-paced
4 Acronym for non-humanities fields
5 Loren who won Best Actress for "Two Women"
6 "___ Me If You Can" (2002 hit film)
7 Editorial slant

	1	2	3	4
5				
6				
7				
8				

ACROSS
1 Pleased
5 Times columnist Frank
6 Largest city in Africa
7 Output of 5-Across and 5-Down
8 "While ___ on the subject . . ."

DOWN
1 Vineyard fruit
2 German gun . . . or a certain winter Olympian
3 Battery end
4 Insult, slangily
5 Times columnist Charles

94

1	2	3	4	5
6				
7				
8				
9				

ACROSS

1 What Britain exited in Brexit
6 Gets better, as a wound
7 ___ the cows come home
8 Van Susteren of NBC News
9 Muscle-to-bone connector

DOWN

1 Tough guys
2 Painter Matisse
3 No longer on one's plate
4 Best of the best
5 What obstruction of justice is part of, informally

ACROSS

1 Chunk of ice
5 Above
6 Caesar or Waldorf
8 "The world's most valuable resource," per The Economist
9 Crossed (out)

DOWN

1 The Red Sox, on scoreboards
2 Get around
3 "Chill out!"
4 Tricky surface for high-heel shoes
7 Family guy

ACROSS

1 "Back in Black" band
5 Common name for a central street
6 Member of the species Homo sapiens
7 What the "U" of UX stands for
8 Count (on)

DOWN

1 Cause to chuckle
2 Saharan transport
3 Blog in book form, essentially
4 Channel known for its countdown clocks
6 "Ben-___"

ACROSS

1 Distant
4 Fingernail shaper
5 See 1-Down
6 "Whoa, calm down!"
7 Crispy sandwich, for short

DOWN

1 With 5-Across, like a trivial problem, colloquially
2 Israel, to the U.S.
3 Like a Triple Word Square in Scrabble
4 Baby horse
5 Baseball glove part

98

ACROSS

1 Owl's question?
4 Spy, slangily
6 Late Bond actor Roger
7 Overturn
8 H.S. equivalency test

DOWN

1 Courted
2 Middle of a steering wheel
3 Gave the green light to
4 A little too pleased with oneself
5 Title for Francis

ACROSS

1 Played the first card
4 Father of Joseph in the Bible
6 Specification in a coffee order
8 Like "The Colbert Report," but not "The Late Show with Stephen Colbert"
9 Prepped
10 Vegas machines
11 "What ___ the chances?"

DOWN

1 Milan opera house
2 Its capital is Quito
3 Injury that a muzzle may prevent
4 Mother ___ (progressive website)
5 Bundles of hay
6 Neither here ___ there
7 Checkers side

1	2	3	4	5
6				
7				
8				
■	9			■

ACROSS

1 Sanskrit term for a yoga position

6 Yoga pose with crossed legs

7 Yoga pose that strengthens the abs

8 Fathers, as a racehorse

9 Bad-mouth

DOWN

1 Europe's largest mountain range

2 Not striped, as a pool ball

3 Video game pioneer that released Asteroids

4 Former California congressman Devin ___

5 Interrogates

ACROSS

1 Sheepskin boot brand
4 Fried chicken piece
7 Masked swordsman of film
8 Banana peel mishap
9 "Heaping" recipe amts.

DOWN

1 Maker of pretzel rods
2 Completely stop texting someone back, in modern lingo
3 HBO show that starred Lena Dunham
5 Hold tightly
6 Brewery ingredient

102

	1	2	3	
4				5
6				
7				
	8			

ACROSS
1 Fidget spinners in 2017, e.g.
4 One of the official languages of the Vatican
6 Symbols that are Japanese for "picture character"
7 Noble gas used in headlights
8 Lair for a bear

DOWN
1 Very well-known
2 Make amends (for)
3 Tangy mustard variety
4 Superman nemesis Luthor
5 Writer Anaïs

	1	2	3	
4				5
6				
7				
8				

ACROSS

1 Dance move with a lowered head in one's bent arm
4 Part of a bike
6 Old enough to participate
7 Seth of 2014's "The Interview"
8 Spines of ships

DOWN

1 Daniel who wrote "Robinson Crusoe"
2 Old saying
3 Cream cheese partner
4 Meat that's both non-kosher and non-halal
5 Word after contact or fisheye

104

1	2	3	4	
5				6
7				
8				
	9			

ACROSS

1 Performs in a play
5 Safe space?
7 Jared Kushner, to the Trump family
8 Music genre associated with a mirrored ball
9 ___ Fifth Avenue

DOWN

1 Enthusiastic
2 ___ Major (Great Dog constellation)
3 Oklahoma city on the Arkansas River
4 Opposite of taut
6 Solid blue balls, in billiards

1	2	3	4	5
6				
7				
8				
9				

ACROSS

1 Becomes frothy
6 Opposite of a liability
7 Cheese, milk, butter, etc.
8 Topic of the "inbox zero" movement
9 Author of the famous line "Abandon all hope, ye who enter here"

DOWN

1 Sun-bleached
2 Target of a 2011 Navy SEAL raid
3 Nepalese or Vietnamese, e.g.
4 Worthiness
5 Do up, as one's hair

106

ACROSS

1 Used to be
4 Mr. or Mrs.
6 ____ Tunnel, Manhattan-to-New Jersey connector
8 Where Sherman's March to the Sea began
9 Avoided, as responsibilities
10 Itching to get started
11 New York baseball player

DOWN

1 Prince who married Kate Middleton
2 Not yet in custody
3 Comfy clothing item that's essentially a backwards robe
4 "Back ____ Future"
5 Type in
6 Owns
7 Honoree on June 18, 2017

	1	2	3	4
5				
6				
7				
8				

ACROSS

1 "Baseball Tonight" channel
5 ___ Ingalls Wilder, author of "Little House on the Prairie"
6 ". . . then again, maybe I'm wrong"
7 Targets of urban renewal
8 "Covfefe" for "coverage," e.g.

DOWN

1 Like the proverbial worm-catching bird
2 Daybreak
3 Teaser ad
4 D.C. baseball team
5 In need of a GPS

108

1	2	3	4	5
6				
7				
8				
■	9			■

ACROSS
1 After his death, Tupac Shakur's were supposedly mixed with marijuana and smoked
6 Horse's closest relative, surprisingly
7 D.C. subway system
8 Do only what he says, in a game
9 Documentarian Burns

DOWN
1 Gives guns to
2 Arab honorific
3 Request for another card in blackjack
4 Energy giant with a spectacular 2001 bankruptcy
5 In the near future

	1	2	3	4
5				
6				
7				
8				

ACROSS

1 Funny, improvised monologue
5 Your ___ (judge's title)
6 Planetary shadow during an eclipse
7 Overly clingy
8 Polytheists believe in them

DOWN

1 Juliet's lover
2 Still under the covers
3 F-150 and Mustang, e.g.
4 Become ragged at the edges
5 Like some juries and paintings

110

ACROSS

1 Jimmy Fallon's network
4 Stock market pessimists
6 Surprise victory
7 Foamy coffee order
8 Curse word cover-up

DOWN

1 Neighbor of China
2 Moisten during roasting
3 Home of the Minotaur's labyrinth
4 Cluster of garlic cloves
5 Bit of choreography

ACROSS

1 Separate, as flour
5 Building material in "The Three Little Pigs"
6 Caribbean nation where voodoo is practiced
7 Miniature map
8 What Adderall treats, for short

DOWN

1 Prepare for the playing of the national anthem
2 Luck of the ____
3 Destined to happen
4 Complete fool
5 Most of Iran, religiously

ACROSS

1 Sound from a hive
4 Film spools
7 Go around the world
8 No ___ for wear
9 Something downloaded with a tap

DOWN

1 Part of the forehead
2 Round number?
3 Serengeti grazer
5 Speak like Daffy Duck
6 Big first for a baby

ACROSS

1 Down
4 Charlotte's home, in children's lit
7 Unicorn of the sea, essentially
9 Attack suddenly and harshly
10 Mouse spotter's cry
11 Lizards sometimes kept as pets
15 Like a budget that's full of cuts
16 Components of the Rockies: Abbr.
17 Sopping

DOWN

1 Noted Trump parodier, for short
2 Bond rating
3 Grinch creator
4 "Huh . . . I had no idea!"
5 ____ de vie (brandy)
6 Nonkosher sandwich
8 Bread choice
11 What "Je suis" translates to
12 Belly
13 "My lips ____ sealed"
14 Place to make a scene?

ACROSS

1 Poetry competition
5 West African country, neighbor of 6-Across
6 West African country, neighbor of 5-Across
7 Appliance with racks
8 The Titanic collided with one

DOWN

1 Jobs in Silicon Valley
2 Antisocial type
3 Growing old
4 The "M" of MTWTF: Abbr.
6 ____ and weave

115

	1	2	3
4			
5			
6			
7			

ACROSS

1 Dot on a domino
4 Tarzan's love
5 Trial figure
6 Trial and ____
7 Russian nos

DOWN

1 San Diego player
2 Gold brick
3 Members of the 4-Down
4 Trial group
5 Brad Pitt's ex, familiarly

ACROSS

1 Card that makes a blackjack with 5-Down
4 Up in the air
6 Film category
7 Noble gas between chlorine and potassium on the periodic table
8 2,000 pounds

DOWN

1 On the lookout
2 African river that's the world's deepest (720 feet)
3 Zac of 2017's "Baywatch"
4 ___ Khan (Turkish title)
5 Card that makes a blackjack with 1-Across

ACROSS

1 Cookie con _ a _ _ er
4 One-named singer with the 2013 #1 hit "Royals"
6 Once more
7 Component of a PowerPoint
8 Female c _ ick _ _

DOWN

1 _ _ _ _ li _ g item for a bride
2 Answer to "Who let the dogs out?"
3 Leakes of reality TV
4 Mascara coats it
5 Look at lasciviously

118

ACROSS

1 Place to learn karate
5 What the Pink Panther is, in the movie "The Pink Panther"
6 Put up with
7 Actress Mila of "Black Swan"
8 Nondairy items often found in the dairy aisle

DOWN

1 Make less likely to crash
2 Needing to pay
3 Luke Skywalker and Obi-Wan Kenobi
4 Shouts to bullfighters
5 Tapper of CNN

ACROSS

1 "Animal Farm" animal
4 It provides the sourness for a whiskey sour
6 Furious
7 Bad thing to run while driving
8 "___ Misérables"

DOWN

1 Danger
2 JPEG file, e.g.
3 Subculture whose members often dressed in black
4 Rapper ___ Yachty
5 Part of a soccer goal

120

ACROSS

1 Mario ____ (racing game)
5 28-year-old singer with over 150 million records sold
7 Snowflake, e.g.
9 Berkeley school, as it's often referred to
10 Brouhaha
11 Stifled laugh
13 Announcement upon arriving
14 Gets the picture

DOWN

1 Green pie ingredient
2 Six-pack set
3 Gets a second chance on a test
4 ____ Joe's
5 Loops into an email discreetly
6 Tehran natives
8 Passed-down tales
12 Michael of "Weekend Update"

ACROSS

1 Breakfast food chain
5 Popular means of communication for long-distance couples
6 Country that's 80% Hindu
7 Doughnut's shape
8 Competed in the first leg of a triathlon

DOWN

1 "Tell me about it"
2 Many-headed serpent slain by Hercules
3 Drug that caused a 1839–42 war
4 Wasabi ___ (spicy snack)
5 Takes a chair

122

	1	2	3	4
5				
6				
7				
8				

ACROSS
1 With 1-Down, overly complimentary article
5 Eatery with booths
6 Like vinyl records, now
7 Getting an A+ on
8 Epitomes of busyness

DOWN
1 See 1-Across
2 Pull some strings?
3 Plants with fiddleheads
4 Kermit, for one
5 Dull-colored

ACROSS

1 Director DuVernay
4 Pesky summer swarm
6 Structure traditionally built by the Inuit
7 One who's always sulking
8 Meg Ryan's repeated shout in an iconic "When Harry Met Sally . . ." scene

DOWN

1 Steamed
2 Hold in high regard
3 Molecule makeup
4 Booking for a band
5 Soak (up)

124

	1	2	3	
4				5
6				
7				
8				

ACROSS

1 & 4 Star of "Wonder Woman"
6 Call off, as a shuttle launch
7 Fret
8 Prepare to propose

DOWN

1 Neighbor of Cameroon
2 Love to pieces
3 Chuck who co-created "Two and a Half Men" and "The Big Bang Theory"
4 Stare unsubtly
5 Texter's "bye for now"

ACROSS

1 "Dear ____ Hansen," Tony-winning musical of 2017
5 Winner of ten French Opens
7 Home of the Burj Khalifa, the world's tallest building
8 Moved stealthily
9 Use a keyboard

DOWN

1 Finales
2 Speak boastfully of
3 Bit of media spending for a company, informally
4 Anti-racism grp. since 1909
6 Facebook button

126

	1	2	3	4
5				
6				
7				
8				

ACROSS

1 With 5-Down, sarcastic round of applause
5 Spicy pepper
6 Root of all Romance languages
7 Advil alternative
8 French father

DOWN

1 Rock targeted in fracking
2 Soda bottle size
3 Greek salad ingredient
4 Sommelier's offering
5 See 1-Across

ACROSS

1 Outlets for internet columnists
6 Double-breasted winter wear
8 Put in other words
9 Roth ____
10 Altoids container
11 Anti-intellectual epithet
13 Hackneyed Instagram photo subjects
14 Past, present or future

DOWN

1 What a six-pack transforms into after too many six packs
2 Layered pasta dish
3 World Series month: Abbr.
4 Facial features of Colonel Sanders and Uncle Sam
5 Make contentedly full
6 Asks nosy questions
7 Works the bar
12 Channel similar to QVC

128

ACROSS
1 Whittled-down pencil
4 Sheet music holder
6 CR-V automaker
7 Get on the last nerve of
8 "Yo"

DOWN
1 Profession for Mrs. Doubtfire and Mary Poppins
2 "Go back" command
3 July 4th, for the U.S.A.
4 Ayatollah's predecessor
5 Muscular firmness

ACROSS

1 What skim milk lacks
4 Greek bread
5 Jordanian "bread"
6 Indian bread
7 ___-C.I.O.

DOWN

1 Championship game
2 ___ angle (skewed)
3 Cigarette substance
4 "La Vie en Rose" singer Edith
5 Its code uses only the letters A, G, C and T

130

	1	2	3	4
5				
6				
7				
8				■

ACROSS

1 Chill (with)
5 Cut off
6 Lewis Carroll title character
7 Like puff pastries and mica rock
8 Years upon years

DOWN

1 Adele song with the lyric "I'm in California dreaming about who we used to be"
2 Bird-related
3 Parts of beer bottles
4 ___ Poupon
5 Umpire's cry

ACROSS

1 Nickname for someone who's 6-foot-5 and 150 pounds, maybe
5 Musical finale
6 & 7 Golfer with 15 major championship wins
8 Clip-___ (some ties)

DOWN

1 Offspring
2 Nike's swoosh and Apple's apple
3 Carded at the bar
4 Home of the invaders in Wells's "The War of the Worlds"
6 Number under @ on a keyboard

132

1	2	3	4	5
6				
7				
8				
9				

ACROSS
1 Vision-related
6 The Everglades, e.g.
7 Wipe off the blackboard
8 The "Homo" in Homo sapiens
9 Donkeys

DOWN
1 Last letter of the Greek alphabet
2 Cuts the rind off
3 Like actress Laverne Cox of "Orange is the New Black"
4 One of Us?
5 Game played on a 64-square board

ACROSS

1 Unexpected problem
5 Home Depot rival
7 Look forward to
8 First name among 2016 Republican presidential candidates
9 "That hurts a lot!"

DOWN

1 Shut angrily
2 "Get outta town!"
3 In the know
4 Insurer known for its funny ads
6 Place in the overhead compartment

134

ACROSS

1 Lampoon
5 Tie the knot
6 Podcast spun off of "This American Life"
7 Company known for its paint swatches
8 One-eighth slice
9 Distraction for a driver
10 Indian dress

DOWN

1 Cocktail that E.B. White called "the elixir of quietude"
2 Orange-and-black bird
3 Construction site sight
4 NASCAR driver Busch
5 Wise teacher
6 "Borat" creator ___ Baron Cohen
7 Nickname for Dad

1	2	3	4	■
5				6
7				
8				
■	9			

ACROSS

1 Walk after an ankle sprain, say
5 Sign when a TV studio is live
7 It creates a buzz in the music world
8 River that lends its name to the second most populous country in the world
9 The Big ___ (New Orleans)

DOWN

1 Mischievous Norse god
2 Foolish
3 Major Japanese automaker
4 Very devout
6 Pink, as cheeks

136

1	2	3	4	
5				6
7				
8				
	9			

ACROSS

1 Designer Jacobs
5 Slightly outdo
7 Part of a drum kit
8 Tennis game start
9 Marvel Comics mutants

DOWN

1 Tree trunk growth
2 Take on new territory, as Russia did with Crimea
3 Furnish with new weapons
4 Parabola, for one
6 Rounded part of a hammer

ACROSS

1 Roald Dahl book, with "The"
4 Cash drawers
6 Scare
7 Singer Katy with the 2010 #1 hit "Firework"
8 Independence ___

DOWN

1 Any two-legged creature
2 Plant life
3 Old ___ (U.S. flag)
4 Recipe amt.
5 Where fireworks burst

138

1	2	3		
4			5	6
7				
8				
	9			

ACROSS

1 What print books have that Kindles lack
4 Boxing matches
7 Narendra Modi's country
8 Donut purchase
9 "It's no ___!"

DOWN

1 Latin abbr. seen in footnote citations
2 It's just simply not done
3 Invasive Japanese vine
5 What overtime periods resolve
6 Mentally with it

	1	2	3	4
	5			
6				
7				
8				

ACROSS

1 Beginning of an idea
5 Super, slangily
6 Sauce often used to top fried fish
7 Forearm bone
8 River in the Greek underworld

DOWN

1 "____ has very quick ears to an accusation": Henry Fielding
2 Ivory's partner
3 Kick back
4 Hospital test that's tough for claustrophobics
6 Land Down Under: Abbr.

140

ACROSS

1 Mercury, Venus or Mars, but not Earth
4 Sweat-inducing, as weather
6 Big concert venue
7 Sweat-inducing, as weather
8 Put into words

DOWN

1 Spiritual teachers
2 Horseshoe-shaped Greek letter
3 Run-down
4 Western omelet meat
5 Midnight to midnight

ACROSS

1 Hoax
5 Headed over now
8 Neighbor of Georgia and Turkey
9 Staring salaciously
10 Gets through deduction, as a math formula
11 Like a small garage
12 Quayle and Aykroyd

DOWN

1 ___ time (something a parent may limit)
2 Hit it out of the park
3 It's celebrated on July 4th
4 Vehicle for a soccer mom
6 San Fran football team
7 Practical jokes
8 Store specializing in shoes and handbags

142

ACROSS

1 Selection when buying plane tickets
5 Resident of Mecca or Medina
6 Hearing-related
7 Garden statue
8 Back talk

DOWN

1 Hot spot in a spa
2 They've replaced marks and francs
3 Thomas Jefferson was his vice president
4 Mah-jongg piece
5 Droops

ACROSS

1 Three-ingredient sandwich
4 Wear for the queen
6 Diet that excludes all processed foods
7 Angry, with "up"
8 W.S.J. alternative

DOWN

1 Scarecrow's wish in "The Wizard of Oz"
2 Candy on a stick, to Brits
3 Bit of birdsong
4 Revival technique
5 Silent assent

144

ACROSS

1 Show stopper?
5 ___ Week, LGBTQ celebration
6 Singer with the 2017 #1 album "Melodrama"
7 Running track shapes
8 Brazilian soccer legend

DOWN

1 Treasure cache
2 Spreading wildly, as an internet video
3 Confuse
4 Almost-failing grades
5 Sound of a frog jumping into a pond

ACROSS

1 Word after Club or before school
4 Swim with the fishes?
6 Sharp-toothed eel
7 Green-lights
8 Toothpaste, e.g.

DOWN

1 Piece of art on a building
2 Site with a "Shop by Category" button
3 Calendar squares
4 Urban pollution
5 Rum + _____ = Cuba Libre

146

ACROSS

1 Honeybee home
5 Time to set an out-of-office message, slangily
6 Bumbling
7 No longer crisp, as potato chips
8 Top-of-the-line

DOWN

1 Bel ___ (singing style)
2 Nearly three quarters of the earth's surface
3 Tree that produces syrup
4 Computer memory unit
5 Immigration document

ACROSS

1 Baby cow
5 Cuban leader succeeded by his brother Raúl
6 Plant used to make tequila
7 "I Know Why the ___ Bird Sings"
8 Home for an arboreal animal

DOWN

1 Thick smoke
2 Proverb
3 Flood preventer
4 Ran away
5 Something found on the inside of a Snapple cap

148

ACROSS
1 Senator Cruz
4 ___ grigio (wine)
6 Animal in a "tuxedo"
8 Like ESPN, Comedy Central and Nickelodeon
9 Color of Hester Prynne's "A"
10 Boneless chicken pieces
11 Word repeated in the lyric "From ___ to shining ___"

DOWN
1 They're tied to the back of a married couple's car
2 Fencing challenge
3 Pro baseball level for the Trenton Thunder and Erie SeaWolves
4 Vice president after Biden
5 Bathroom floor installer
6 Facebook page entry
7 Trawling equipment

1	2	3	4	5
6				
7				
8				
9				

ACROSS

1 Public perception, so to speak
6 "Copy that"
7 Faulkner's "A Rose for ___"
8 2008 Pixar film about a robot
9 Villain's look of contempt

DOWN

1 Beers, slangily
2 Citizen under Caesar
3 Nimble
4 "In the," in Italian
5 Machine next to a washer

150

ACROSS

1 Tom Brady and Aaron Rodgers: Abbr.
4 Disney film with the song "I'll Make a Man Out of You"
6 Get back together, as alumni
7 Opposite of wordy
8 Org. with guards and shooters

DOWN

1 Powerful chess piece
2 Book jacket promo
3 Eldest Stark daughter on "Game of Thrones"
4 Mohawk-sporting actor
5 Born, in marriage announcements

ANSWERS

1

	M	A	C	Y	S
	B	I	L	L	O	W
V	E	S	T	I	G	E
A	C	T		M	U	D
D	O	I	C	A	R	E
E	M	M	I	T	T	
R	E	E	S	E		

2

	C	L	E	F
	L	U	N	A
B	A	N	J	O
E	R	G	O	
E	A	S	Y	

3

	U	F	O	S
	T	U	R	F
D	U	N	N	O
A	R	G	O	
S	N	I	T	

4

A	S	A	P	█
L	A	P	S	E
A	L	P	H	A
S	O	L	A	R
█	N	E	W	S

5

J	A	P	A	N
C	R	E	P	E
O	B	E	S	E
L	O	V	E	D
E	R	E	█	█

6

█	Q	T	I	P
C	U	R	V	E
Y	O	U	I	N
A	T	S	E	A
N	E	T	S	█

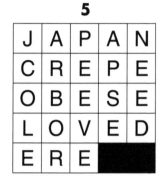

7

	T	H	A	I
	W	I	N	D
J	E	N	G	A
U	R	D	U	
S	K	I	S	

8

		M	O	P		
	B	Y	R	O	N	
C	R	A	D	L	E	D
H	U	N		E	P	I
A	L	M	A	N	A	C
S	E	A	T	T	L	E
M	E	R	M	A	I	D

9

	N	S	A	
M	O	U	T	H
A	D	E	L	E
S	U	D	A	N
	H	E	S	

10

E	P	I	C	■
V	I	N	Y	L
E	X	T	R	A
S	E	R	U	M
■	L	O	S	E

11

■	L	E	D	■
D	E	V	O	S
I	M	A	G	E
N	U	D	G	E
G	R	E	Y	S

12

S	I	G	M	A
O	N	E	A	L
A	C	T	I	I
K	A	T	Z	S
■	N	Y	E	T

13

	E	D	D	Y
	F	R	E	E
P	R	E	S	S
S	O	C	K	
I	N	K	S	

14

	L	A	L	A
M	I	D	I	S
A	B	O	V	E
L	Y	R	I	C
L	A	N	D	

15

B	A	T	H	M	A	T
U	K	R	A	I	N	E
C	A	I	T	L	Y	N
		F	B	I		
P	E	L	O	T	O	N
I	N	E	X	I	L	E
C	D	S		A	D	D

16

T	A	B	S	
I	R	O	N	
N	O	R	A	H
	M	O	R	E
	A	N	K	H

17

		E	B	B
C	O	M	E	Y
A	P	A	R	T
B	E	I	G	E
S	N	L		

18

	S	T	A	Y
	W	O	K	E
G	E	A	R	S
P	E	S	O	
A	T	T	N	

19

P	A	R	K	
D	R	A	M	A
F	E	T	A	L
S	N	O	R	E
	A	N	T	S

20

	O	M	G	
E	V	E	R	Y
R	A	D	I	O
I	T	A	L	Y
C	E	L	L	O

21

C	A	M	E	L
O	B	A	M	A
L	O	G	A	N
T	U	N	I	C
S	T	A	L	E

22

I	R	A	S		
R	U	S	H	E	D
A	N	S	A	R	I
Q	U	E	P	A	S	A
	P	R	I	S	M	S
	S	T	R	E	A	M
		O	R	L	Y

23

A	M	P	
R	A	I	S	E
C	Y	N	I	C
H	O	O	C	H
		T	K	O

24

		C	I	A
B	E	A	S	T
R	U	B	I	O
A	R	I	S	E
N	O	N		

25

	P	E	E	P
B	A	D	G	E
O	B	G	Y	N
S	L	A	P	S
S	O	R	T	

26

	F	L	Y	
F	E	L	I	Z
D	R	A	K	E
R	A	M	E	N
	L	A	S	

27

	L	A	B		
E	X	A	M	S	
A	L	G	A	E	
P	E	E	L	E	
		L	E	D	

28

R	S	V	P	S
A	W	A	R	E
N	O	L	I	E
D	R	U	N	K
B	E	E	T	S

29

		L	E	S	T
	S	I	X	E	R
	H	I	P	P	I	E
B	I	G	B	A	N	K
O	R	N	A	T	E	
T	E	A	L	S		
H	E	L	M			

30

		F	B	I
S	H	O	O	T
C	O	U	R	T
A	L	L	E	Y
N	A	S		

31

E	Y	R	E	
P	O	O	L	
A	U	G	U	R
	R	U	D	E
	S	E	E	D

32

	M	A	C	S
	A	L	O	E
S	L	I	M	E
A	T	O	M	
D	A	N	A	

33

A	C	L	U	
R	H	I	N	O
C	A	T	C	H
H	O	H	U	M
	S	E	T	S

34

F	A	R		
A	L	I	G	N
D	O	G	M	A
E	T	H	O	S
		T	S	A

35

	Z	E	R	O
C	O	D	E	R
A	R	G	U	E
P	R	E	S	S
N	O	S	E	

36

		S	U	V	
	Z	I	P	I	T
L	O	D	G	E	R	S
I	N	E	R	T	I	A
L	E	B	A	N	O	N
	D	A	D	A	S	
		R	E	M		

37

	A	B	S
S	T	I	L	L
H	A	G	U	E
A	C	H	E	D
H	O	T		

38

T	V	S	E	T
H	E	L	L	O
R	E	E	L	S
E	P	E	E	S
E	S	P	N	

39

A	L	I		
N	A	V	Y	
T	R	I	A	D
	D	E	L	I
		S	E	X

40

	B	O	O	T
H	A	L	V	E
I	N	D	E	X
S	T	I	N	T
S	U	E	S	

41

	M	I	L	D
	O	H	I	O
B	R	O	K	E
R	O	P	E	
O	N	E	S	

42

	M	A	C	K
	E	U	R	O
J	A	R	E	D
F	L	A	P	
K	Y	L	E	

43

S	U	I		P	B	S
C	N	N		E	L	I
O	R	D	E	R	I	N
T	E	E	M	I	N	G
T	A	X	C	O	D	E
	D	E	E	D	S	
		D	E	S		

44

45

S	A	L	T	
O	N	I	O	N
P	O	P	P	Y
	N	O	U	N
		S	P	Y

G	I	F	T	
A	C	R	I	D
M	I	A	M	I
Y	E	M	E	N
	R	E	D	O

46

47

S	A	P	P	Y
A	G	R	E	E
G	E	A	R	S
A	N	D	R	E
S	T	A	Y	S

48

49

	S	C	A	M
	C	O	D	E
H	U	R	O	N
A	S	A	P	
J	I	L	T	

50

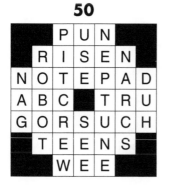

		P	U	N	
	R	I	S	E	N
N	O	T	E	P	A	D
A	B	C		T	R	U
G	O	R	S	U	C	H
	T	E	E	N	S	
	W	E	E		

51

	C	A	B	
N	O	B	E	L
P	R	I	Z	E
R	A	D	O	N
	L	E	S	

52

	N	O	D	
B	E	Z	O	S
F	U	Z	Z	Y
F	R	I	E	S
	O	E	D	

53

A	W	M	A	N
P	R	O	N	E
P	I	N	T	A
S	E	D	E	R
	R	E	D	

54

	F	A	C	E
B	E	L	A	Y
A	D	O	R	E
B	E	N	D	S
E	X	E	S	

55

N	B	A		
A	E	S	O	P
P	E	P	S	I
A	R	E	S	T
		N	O	S

56

E	M	M	A	
G	U	A	V	A
O	S	C	A	R
S	T	O	N	E
	A	N	T	S

57

		A	L	I		
	S	P	A	R	K	
P	O	P	S	O	U	T
O	R	L	A	N	D	O
S	E	A	L	I	O	N
	R	U	L	E	S	
		D	E	S		

58

	A	N	D	
S	T	O	R	M
T	A	B	O	O
A	L	L	O	T
G	L	Y	P	H

59

	A	R	M	S
	W	E	A	K
S	A	U	C	E
I	K	N	E	W
N	E	E	D	S

60

	S	U	M	
C	A	N	O	E
I	D	T	A	G
S	L	I	N	G
	Y	E	A	

61

	B	A	R	N
	R	U	I	N
S	U	R	G	E
U	T	A	H	
V	E	S	T	

62

S	P	O	R	K
C	U	B	A	N
A	G	A	V	E
N	E	M	E	A
S	T	A	N	D

63

O	R	B	I	T
C	H	E	M	O
C	O	L	O	N
U	N	I	F	Y
R	E	E	F	S

64

65

66

67

A	S	H	
B	L	E	E	D
C	I	R	C	A
S	P	E	R	M
		S	U	N

68

	M	A	D	E
	A	L	A	S
T	U	L	I	P
I	R	I	S	
N	Y	N	Y	

69

C	A	S	E	S
A	P	P	L	E
F	R	U	I	T
F	I	R	T	H
E	L	S	E	

70

D	I	A	L	
A	C	R	E	
Y	A	R	D	S
	L	A	T	E
	L	Y	O	N

71

		S	E	T		
	M	U	S	I	C	
C	A	N	C	E	R	S
O	C	D		I	A	M
A	R	I	A	N	N	A
T	O	A	S	T	E	R
S	N	L	H	O	S	T

72

O	W	L	S	
C	H	A	O	S
T	E	S	L	A
O	L	S	E	N
	P	O	S	E

73

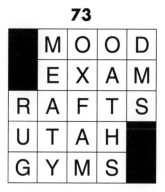

	M	O	O	D
	E	X	A	M
R	A	F	T	S
U	T	A	H	
G	Y	M	S	

74

D	U	M	B	
U	B	E	R	
D	O	D	O	S
	L	I	N	K
	T	A	X	I

75

	N	U	T	
O	A	S	I	S
N	I	H	A	O
E	V	E	R	Y
	E	R	A	

76

	S	I	X	
T	A	D	A	S
A	L	E	X	A
G	M	A	I	L
S	A	L	S	A

77

	S	K	A	
B	E	A	N	S
B	O	U	G	H
Q	U	A	S	H
	L	I	T	

78

	O	P	I	N	E	
	M	I	N	E	R	
S	E	T	B	A	I	L
A	L	B	E	R	T	A
N	E	U	T	E	R	S
A	T	L	A	S	E	S
A	S	L		T	A	O

79

	B	E	A	R
J	O	L	L	Y
U	N	I	T	E
J	U	D	A	S
U	S	E	R	

80

M	E	O	W	S
S	Q	U	A	T
N	U	T	S	O
B	A	D	P	R
C	L	O	S	E

81

S	A	G		
P	H	O	T	O
A	C	T	O	R
M	A	Y	A	S
		A	D	O

82

	G	U	F	F
W	A	Z	O	O
I	M	B	U	E
F	E	E	L	S
I	R	K	S	

83

	F	L	A	G
C	A	I	R	O
A	N	V	I	L
S	T	E	E	D
E	A	R	S	

84

N	A	D	A	L
A	L	O	N	E
S	O	N	I	A
T	H	U	M	P
Y	A	T	E	S

85

	D	E	A	T	H	
A	R	R	I	V	A	L
G	E	O	R	G	I	A
H	S	T		U	R	N
A	S	I	N	I	N	E
S	E	C	E	D	E	S
	S	A	G	E	T	

86

	P	J	S	
F	L	U	K	Y
A	U	D	I	E
S	M	E	L	L
T	B	A	L	L

87

	G	O	A	T
	U	N	D	O
H	I	T	U	P
E	L	A	L	
W	E	P	T	

88

E	D	G	E	
M	A	R	X	
S	T	I	F	F
	E	L	B	A
	S	L	I	T

89

	O	H	M	
O	N	E	A	M
W	I	N	C	E
L	O	C	A	L
	N	E	W	

90

	S	W	A	Y
	H	A	H	A
F	I	V	E	K
A	R	E	A	
N	E	R	D	

91

92

93

94

T	H	E	E	U
H	E	A	L	S
U	N	T	I	L
G	R	E	T	A
S	I	N	E	W

95

96

97

98

99

100

A	S	A	N	A
L	O	T	U	S
P	L	A	N	K
S	I	R	E	S
■	D	I	S	■

101

U	G	G	■	
T	H	I	G	H
Z	O	R	R	O
■	S	L	I	P
	T	S	P	S

102

■	F	A	D	■
L	A	T	I	N
E	M	O	J	I
X	E	N	O	N
■	D	E	N	■

103

	D	A	B	
P	E	D	A	L
O	F	A	G	E
R	O	G	E	N
K	E	E	L	S

104

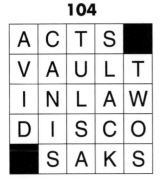

A	C	T	S	
V	A	U	L	T
I	N	L	A	W
D	I	S	C	O
	S	A	K	S

105

F	O	A	M	S
A	S	S	E	T
D	A	I	R	Y
E	M	A	I	L
D	A	N	T	E

106

	W	A	S		
	T	I	T	L	E
H	O	L	L	A	N	D
A	T	L	A	N	T	A
S	H	I	R	K	E	D
	E	A	G	E	R	
	M	E	T		

107

	E	S	P	N
L	A	U	R	A
O	R	N	O	T
S	L	U	M	S
T	Y	P	O	

108

A	S	H	E	S
R	H	I	N	O
M	E	T	R	O
S	I	M	O	N
	K	E	N	

109

	R	I	F	F
H	O	N	O	R
U	M	B	R	A
N	E	E	D	Y
G	O	D	S	

110

	N	B	C	
B	E	A	R	S
U	P	S	E	T
L	A	T	T	E
B	L	E	E	P

111

	S	I	F	T
S	T	R	A	W
H	A	I	T	I
I	N	S	E	T
A	D	H	D	

112

B	Z	Z		
R	E	E	L	S
O	R	B	I	T
W	O	R	S	E
		A	P	P

113

S	A	D		W	E	B
N	A	R	W	H	A	L
L	A	S	H	O	U	T
		E	E	K		
I	G	U	A	N	A	S
A	U	S	T	E	R	E
M	T	S		W	E	T

114

	S	L	A	M
	T	O	G	O
B	E	N	I	N
O	V	E	N	
B	E	R	G	

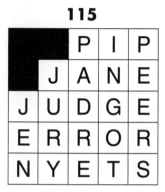

115

	P	I	P
	J	A	N	E
J	U	D	G	E
E	R	R	O	R
N	Y	E	T	S

116

	A	C	E	
A	L	O	F	T
G	E	N	R	E
A	R	G	O	N
	T	O	N	

117

	T	I	N
L	O	R	D	E
A	G	A	I	N
S	L	I	D	E
H	E	N	

118

	D	O	J	O
J	E	W	E	L
A	B	I	D	E
K	U	N	I	S
E	G	G	S	

119

	P	I	G	
L	E	M	O	N
I	R	A	T	E
L	I	G	H	T
	L	E	S	

120

		K	A	R	T	
	B	I	E	B	E	R
C	R	Y	S	T	A	L
C	A	L		A	D	O
S	N	I	C	K	E	R
	I	M	H	E	R	E
	S	E	E	S		

121

122

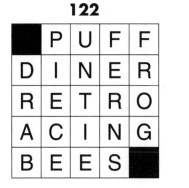

123

124

	G	A	L	
G	A	D	O	T
A	B	O	R	T
W	O	R	R	Y
K	N	E	E	L

125

E	V	A	N	
N	A	D	A	L
D	U	B	A	I
S	N	U	C	K
	T	Y	P	E

126

	S	L	O	W
C	H	I	L	I
L	A	T	I	N
A	L	E	V	E
P	E	R	E	

127

	B	L	O	G	S	
P	E	A	C	O	A	T
R	E	S	T	A	T	E
I	R	A		T	I	N
E	G	G	H	E	A	D
S	U	N	S	E	T	S
	T	E	N	S	E	

128

		N	U	B
S	T	A	N	D
H	O	N	D	A
A	N	N	O	Y
H	E	Y		

129

		F	A	T
	P	I	T	A
D	I	N	A	R
N	A	A	N	
A	F	L		

130

	H	A	N	G
S	E	V	E	R
A	L	I	C	E
F	L	A	K	Y
E	O	N	S	

131

	S	L	I	M
	C	O	D	A
T	I	G	E	R
W	O	O	D	S
O	N	S		

132

O	P	T	I	C
M	A	R	S	H
E	R	A	S	E
G	E	N	U	S
A	S	S	E	S

133

S	N	A	G	
L	O	W	E	S
A	W	A	I	T
M	A	R	C	O
	Y	E	O	W

134

		M	O	C	K
	M	A	R	R	Y
	S	E	R	I	A	L
P	A	N	T	O	N	E
O	C	T	I	L	E
P	H	O	N	E
S	A	R	I

135

L	I	M	P	
O	N	A	I	R
K	A	Z	O	O
I	N	D	U	S
	E	A	S	Y

136

M	A	R	C	
O	N	E	U	P
S	N	A	R	E
S	E	R	V	E
	X	M	E	N

137

	B	F	G	
T	I	L	L	S
S	P	O	O	K
P	E	R	R	Y
	D	A	Y	

138

I	N	K		
B	O	U	T	S
I	N	D	I	A
D	O	Z	E	N
		U	S	E

139

	G	E	R	M
	U	B	E	R
A	I	O	L	I
U	L	N	A	
S	T	Y	X	

140

	G	O	D	
H	U	M	I	D
A	R	E	N	A
M	U	G	G	Y
	S	A	Y	

141

	S	H	A	M	
	C	O	M	I	N	G
A	R	M	E	N	I	A
L	E	E	R	I	N	G
D	E	R	I	V	E	S
O	N	E	C	A	R	
		D	A	N	S	

142

	S	E	A	T
S	A	U	D	I
A	U	R	A	L
G	N	O	M	E
S	A	S	S	

143

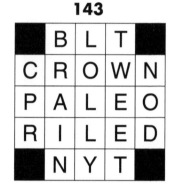

	B	L	T	
C	R	O	W	N
P	A	L	E	O
R	I	L	E	D
	N	Y	T	

144

	T	V	A	D
P	R	I	D	E
L	O	R	D	E
O	V	A	L	S
P	E	L	E	

145

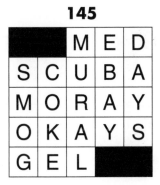

	M	E	D	
S	C	U	B	A
M	O	R	A	Y
O	K	A	Y	S
G	E	L		

146

	C	O	M	B
V	A	C	A	Y
I	N	E	P	T
S	T	A	L	E
A	O	N	E	

147

	C	A	L	F
F	I	D	E	L
A	G	A	V	E
C	A	G	E	D
T	R	E	E	

148

		T	E	D		
	P	I	N	O	T	
P	E	N	G	U	I	N
O	N	C	A	B	L	E
S	C	A	R	L	E	T
T	E	N	D	E	R	S
		S	E	A		

149

B	R	A	N	D
R	O	G	E	R
E	M	I	L	Y
W	A	L	L	E
S	N	E	E	R

150

	Q	B	S	
M	U	L	A	N
R	E	U	N	E
T	E	R	S	E
	N	B	A	

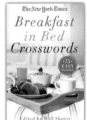

Looking for more Hard Crosswords?

The New York Times

The #1 Name in Crosswords

Looking for more Large-Print Crosswords?

The New York Times

The #1 Name in Crosswords

Looking for more Sunday Crosswords?

The New York Times

The #1 Name in Crosswords

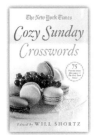

Available at your local bookstore or online at nytimes.com/store/books

St. Martin's Griffin